BR Railfreight

...off the beaten track

Volume 1

**Merseyside, Greater Manchester,
Lancashire and Cheshire;
Derbyshire, Nottinghamshire,
Yorkshire and Humberside**

A Photographic Journey

from the camera of

Peter Hill

Copyright Freightline Publications

© **May 1991**

**Produced for the Publishers by
Mopok Graphics, Glossop, Derbyshire.
Distribution by Transport Publishing Co Ltd
128 Pikes Lane, Glossop, Derbyshire
Trade Enquiries: 0457.861508**

Introduction

Freight workings are an integral part of the BR network, and bring in vital revenue to a railway that must be the most financially neglected in Europe. Successive governments have invested heavily in road construction schemes which have made the railway a poor relation when it comes down to injections of cash!

Sectorisation within BR has helped to 'balance the books' and it is pleasing to see that the Railfreight arm of BR has vastly improved efficiency in the various sub-sectors. However what is alarming was BR's decision on 12th December 1990 to abandon and close the Speedlink Network from 8th July 1991.

The first Speedlink working was introduced in 1973 between Bristol and Glasgow. The service was to expand, and eventually linked nineteen major centres within Britain, giving Railfreight customers a first class service.

By the early 1980s Britain was in the grip of a recession which meant the closure of many marshalling yards and terminals which were serviced by Speedlink. In 1990 just eight main yards survived, including Warrington Arpley and Doncaster Belmont, the traffic patterns of which are covered in the course of this book.

The whole Speedlink operation had been reviewed in the late 1980s when Freightliner and Speedlink were combined to form Railfreight Distribution. During the review it was found that not one single Speedlink flow was showing a profit, and with much of the wagon and loco fleets needing replacement because of old age the writing was on the wall.

The major effect of the Speedlink loss in general public terms will be seen by the increased amount of traffic, particularly heavy lorries, on our already congested road systems. But with governments of the day investing heavily in roads rather than rail, this outcome is not unexpected.

Not all is doom and gloom, however. When Speedlink is finally laid to rest in July 1991, rail managers hope to retain at least some of the traffic flows in the form of block trains.

The object of this book was to take a pictorial look at locations which could quite well disappear with the closure of Speedlink. I have concentrated on various types of traffic, including Speedlink as well as other Railfreight sub-sector workings.

These could involve a Railfreight Petroleum block oil train at Immingham or a Railfreight Distribution trip working at Hindlow on the truncated and isolated Ashbourne line in Derbyshire. A Class 47 along with a driver and shunter to pick up a single tank from a chemical works on a truncated branch line simply has not made Speedlink pay.

Geographically the book covers a band of northern England extending between Liverpool Docks and Immingham Docks with such major centres as Manchester, Preston, Leeds, Sheffield and Doncaster included. Also highlighted are very much 'OFF THE BEATEN TRACK' locations.

Included are pictures of the Haydock Branch, Bickershaw Colliery, Fiddlers Ferry, Folly Lane branch, Partington, Glazebrook, Oakleigh, Westhoughton, Burn Naze, Peak Forest, Shirebrook, Barrow Hill, the South Yorkshire Joint Railway system, Treeton Junction, Thorpe Marsh Power Station, Deepcar, Royston Junction, Knottingley, Scunthorpe and Grimsby Docks, to name several.

Finally thanks must go to my parents, Kathleen and Leonard Hill, and Ron Martin for their understanding and help during the compilation of this book.

Peter Hill
Standish, Wigan
May 1991

For Daniel, Oliver and Tom, pictured left at March MPD

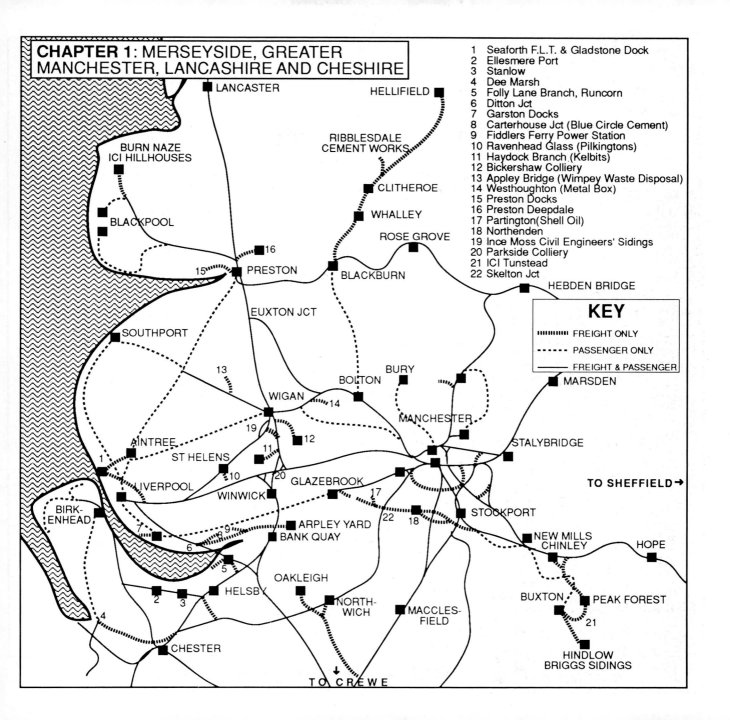

CHAPTER 1: MERSEYSIDE, GREATER MANCHESTER, LANCASHIRE AND CHESHIRE

1 Seaforth F.L.T. & Gladstone Dock
2 Ellesmere Port
3 Stanlow
4 Dee Marsh
5 Folly Lane Branch, Runcorn
6 Ditton Jct
7 Garston Docks
8 Carterhouse Jct (Blue Circle Cement)
9 Fiddlers Ferry Power Station
10 Ravenhead Glass (Pilkingtons)
11 Haydock Branch (Kelbits)
12 Bickershaw Colliery
13 Appley Bridge (Wimpey Waste Disposal)
14 Westhoughton (Metal Box)
15 Preston Docks
16 Preston Deepdale
17 Partington (Shell Oil)
18 Northenden
19 Ince Moss Civil Engineers' Sidings
20 Parkside Colliery
21 ICI Tunstead
22 Skelton Jct

KEY

▬▬▬▬	FREIGHT ONLY
- - - -	PASSENGER ONLY
▬▬▬	FREIGHT & PASSENGER

LANCASTER
HELLIFIELD
RIBBLESDALE CEMENT WORKS
BURN NAZE ICI HILLHOUSES
CLITHEROE
WHALLEY
BLACKPOOL
ROSE GROVE
16
PRESTON
15
BLACKBURN
EUXTON JCT
HEBDEN BRIDGE
SOUTHPORT
BURY
13
BOLTON
MARSDEN
WIGAN
14
AINTREE
19
MANCHESTER
ST HELENS
11
12
STALYBRIDGE
1
10
20
GLAZEBROOK
LIVERPOOL
WINWICK
17
TO SHEFFIELD →
BIRK-ENHEAD
22
18
STOCKPORT
7
ARPLEY YARD
9
NEW MILLS
8
BANK QUAY
CHINLEY
HOPE
6
5
OAKLEIGH
BUXTON
PEAK FOREST
2
3
HELSBY
21
NORTH-WICH
MACCLES-FIELD
4
CHESTER
HINDLOW BRIGGS SIDINGS

TO CREWE

TOP LEFT: 47112, a member of Tinsley's Railfreight Distribution fleet (FDAT), crosses Liverpool's Dock Road at 06.00 on the morning of the 29th June 1990, its container wagons highlighted by the low sun rising from the east. 47112, in the old Railfreight livery of grey bodysides, yellow cabs, and red buffer beams, is running nearly one hour early as the 4F51 from Garston Freightliner Terminal to Seaforth FLT, and is conveying containers for export via Liverpool Docks. They had arrived at Garston from Stratford, East London, the previous evening. Seaforth receives one regular working each day from Garston in order to connect with sailings from the docks. The morning working is booked to leave Garston at 06.45 and returns from Seaforth at 18.15 as the 4K49 to Crewe. The ex-Lancashire and Yorkshire Bootle branch over which the Freightliner traffic travels has seen an upsurge in workings since 1988 with imported coal arriving, firstly, from America and latterly, from Columbia, in 60,000 tonne ships. The coal is rail-removed from Gladstone Docks and is destined for Fiddlers Ferry Power Station near Warrington. At present two pairs of Class 20s are used to haul 45 HAA hoppers up the 1 in 60 gradient from Alexandra Dock goods yard, now disused, to Bootle Junction. During July 1990, however, a pair of Class 56 coal sector locos were involved in trials on the branch and during December 1990 Class 60s were involved with test trains hauling 45 HAAs up the dock branch to Edge Hill. With drivers now being trained at Springs Branch depot, Wigan, on Class 60s, the end must be in sight for Class 20s on this work.

CENTRE LEFT: 08939 is pictured in Ditton Yard on the 22nd June 1990 shunting Civil Engineer's permanent way wagons in readiness for weekend work in the Liverpool area. On the left of 08939, a member of Allerton's FSMA shunter fleet is a rake of empty PCA cement wagons which had earlier been tripped up from the Blue Circle Cement Terminal at Tanhouse Lane, Widnes. They are destined for Blue Circle's complex at Earles Sidings, Hope. They will leave Ditton as the 6H33 SO working and will be hauled to Hope by a Class 37. This service also operates on a Wednesday and Friday with loaded PCA tanks arriving back at Ditton from Earles Sidings on a Tuesday and Thursday running as the 6F59. PCAs can also arrive at Ditton Yard from Eastgate located to the north-west of Bishop Auckland.

LOWER LEFT: For a period during 1988-89, 86258 *Talyllyn, The First Preserved Railway*, was renumbered to 86501 and became part of a dedicated fleet of eight Class 86 locomotives which were regeared and restricted to 75mph for exclusive use on Freightliner services. However, this experiment was short-lived and during 1989, 86501 was renumbered back to 86258 and now forms part of the Inter City Cross Country fleet of engines (ICCA), again running at 100mph on passenger workings. In its old guise, 86501 in the old Inter City livery is pictured at Garston Junction on the 21st June 1988 waiting to leave with the 4L85 Freightliner service to Dagenham. The Guinness containers which can be seen behind the loco have been tripped from Spekeland Road, and will be detached at Willesden to return empty to Park Royal Brewery, London. Other containers in the train will eventually be exported via Felixstowe Docks. Garston also helps dispatch the 6L42 Ford Company train from Halewood to Dagenham each weekday. The Ford group have recently celebrated 25 years of car production on Merseyside and BR Railfreight Distribution have acknowledged this fact by naming loco 47309 *The Halewood Transmission*. British Rail have themselves been involved with the Ford trains for a quarter of a century! The ex-LNWR Garston Docks also deal with coal export traffic to Ireland, mainly from Toton. There is some Speedlink traffic dealt with, albeit on an irregular basis from the Metalbox Company sidings in Aintree.

TOP RIGHT: 08402 is a trip shunter allocated to Allerton depot, and may be seen in the same day at locations which can include Runcorn, Widnes or Ditton. With the River Mersey in the background the shunter is pictured at the ICI sidings, Folly Lane, Runcorn. These large sidings run off a spur from the main Liverpool to Crewe line at Runcorn station. Folly Lane can despatch up to eight company trains a week and three locations down the branch are rail-served, namely the docks, and the ICI works at Weston and Castner-Kellner. 08402 is shunting ICI Mond tanks ready for a company train to Haverton Hill on Teeside. The date of the picture is the 22nd June 1990. 08402 was originally D3517 and built by BR at Darlington Works.

LOWER RIGHT: I make no apologies for using this sentimental picture of Aintree steam shed (27B, 8L) which actually closed in 1967 but still remains standing in June 1990. However, it would be impossible for locos to use the depot today as the permanent way was removed years ago and 'Mother Nature' has since taken over. A far cry from the days when Aintree played host to visiting Britannia Pacific steam engines on Grand National specials. The only track left in this area today is the freight spur from Bootle Junction which serves the private sidings of the Metalbox Company situated in Aintree. Traffic on this branch runs on an 'as required' basis and is rare, to say the least. During the depot's last few years of life, shunters in the form of the diminutive Class 02s were based at Aintree for work in the nearby Liverpool Docks.

ABOVE: 37072, still in Standard BR blue livery, storms passed the Albright and Wilson Chemical works in Widnes as it approaches Tanhouse Lane on the freight-only line from Ditton Junction to Warrington Arpley with the 6T65 working containing three POA scrap wagons from Ford's Halewood Plant. The scrap is destined for Tinsley Yard, Sheffield, and will run forward from Arpley Yard as the 6E63. 37072 is now in BR General livery, plain grey with black cab doors and is a member of Cardiff Canton's FPEK fleet of Petroleum locos. This busy section of freight line is also used by the Gladstone Dock to Fiddlers Ferry imported-coal trains hauled by a pair of Class 20s. The various sidings at Widnes West Deviation yard to the west of Tanhouse Lane are now sadly disused, their traffic being transferred to Ditton Yard and then tripped onto the Speedlink Yard at Warrington Arpley. 37072 when pictured on the 23rd August 1988 was allocated to Tinsley and was then part of the depot's Departmental Civil Engineer's Western Fleet.

UPPER RIGHT FACING: Passing the green algae-covered St Helens canal at Carterhouse Junction signalbox, Widnes, are 20120 in BR blue livery and 20090 in early Railfreight livery which incorporated a red solebar. They are working the 7R67 Gladstone Docks to Fiddlers Ferry imported American coal MGR train which conveys 30 HAA hoppers. In the background is the ICI paraquat plant which forms part of a large ICI complex situated on the northern banks of the River Mersey. The plant is rail-connected but at the time of writing generates little traffic.

WIDNES

LOWER RIGHT FACING: 08402, in ex-works condition and sporting its overall grey livery, shunts trip T69 which consists of PCA cement tanks at the Blue Circle's Widnes depot in Tanhouse Lane. The spur to the cement depot was opened from Carterhouse Junction in 1981. The empty PCAs will be tripped to Ditton Yard, over ex-LNWR metals, by 08402, and will eventually form the 6H33 to Blue Circle's Earles Sidings complex at Hope in the Peak District. To the right is a rake of TTA tanks which are bound for Stanlow. The Blue Circle depot receives one trip working of PCAs each day and the TTAs are returned to Stanlow once a week. They carry fuel oil for the company's large road haulage fleet as well as heating oil. 08402 is based at Allerton and is part of the FSMA fleet. The line between Ditton Junction and Warrington Arpley, now freight only, lost its passenger services on the 15th September 1958 when the stations at Sankey Bridges, Fiddlers Ferry and Penketh closed. Today of course Fiddlers Ferry is well known for its power station which is served by MGR coal trains from both Lancashire and Yorkshire as well as the Point of Ayr colliery in North Wales.

ABOVE: 47233 *Strombidae*, when pictured a Railfreight Crewe Petroleum pool engine (FPBC) but now belonging to the Eastfield Petroleum pool (FPAE), waits for 08402 to shunt its train, the 6T65 trip to Warrington Arpley yard. It contains caustic soda tanks from ICI Weston situated on the Folly Lane branch. Between the two locos can be seen Runcorn Transporter Bridge constructed in the early '60s to replace an older bridge which linked the towns of Widnes and Runcorn. The Folly Lane branch is electrified but today only diesel traction uses the branch, the last electric train running during 1985 to Willesden in north London.

LEFT: 31163 an Immingham-allocated Railfreight Petroleum loco (FPCI) is pictured drifting down the Haydock branch at Ashton-in-Makerfield, near Wigan, with the early morning 7M25 (TTHo) arrival of TTA tanks from Lindsey Oil Refinery, Immingham. The train is servicing the Kelbits bitumen plant located at the end of the short spur to the left of the picture. The working gains access to the WCML during its journey from Humberside via Lowton Junction, and then runs up to Springs Branch depot where the loco runs round. The train is propelled into the Kelbits plant, and on leaving the premises runs round again to join the WCML in a northerly direction. When the train reaches Springs Branch about two miles away, another run-round occurs and the train proceeds in a southerly direction to Lowton Junction. The Haydock branch, an ex-Great Central line, which used to run from Glazebrook to the original St Helens Central Station is now truncated at Haydock Park Race Course Station. Until two years ago the Lowton Metal sidings were also served on the branch, but this firm has now closed and Kelbits is the only reason the branch remains open.

UPPER RIGHT: In this picture taken at British Coal's Parkside complex, 20010, one of the first of the Class to be repainted into the original Railfreight livery, is partnered with 20082, both being members of Toton's FEGN fleet. When the HAA hoppers have been loaded the train will depart as the 7T76 to Fiddlers Ferry, a relatively new Power Station opened in 1969. Note the bulldozer on the left of the picture which carries the loose coal onto a conveyer belt system which transfers it up into the waiting HAAs. When all the hoppers are full the locos will run round for the journey to Fiddlers Ferry.

PARKSIDE COLLIERY

LOWER RIGHT: Lancashire can still boast two rail connected collieries, at Bickershaw near Leigh, and Parkside situated in Newton le Willows. It is here that Class 20s, 20169 and 20045 both in original BR blue livery are pictured travelling at ½ mph under the rapid loader. The ageing Class 20s are allocated to Toton's Railfreight Power Station Coal North-West loco fleet (FEGN) which are outstabled at Springs Branch depot, Wigan. However, since the photograph was taken on 23rd September 1990, 20045 has been withdrawn and 20169 now belongs to the FEFN fleet. Springs Branch carries out A and B exams on its remaining Class 20s, the A exam taking place after 55 hours. 20169 and 20045 were working the 7T79 to Fiddlers Ferry. Access to the main Manchester to Liverpool line is by a spur, and at Earlestown the train will head south to Warrington Arpley Yard. Here an 08 shunter will be attached at the rear of the working and the whole formation will be dragged onto the freight-only line between Arpley and Ditton Junction. After this movement the Class 20s will head the train to Fiddlers Ferry Power Station. Parkside despatches two trains per day to Fiddlers Ferry, including one Sunday afternoon departure.

UPPER LEFT: Class 45, 45104 *The Royal Warwickshire Fusiliers*, is pictured at Ince Moss Civil Engineer's sidings which lie to the north of the Wigan North-Western to Liverpool Lime Street line close to Springs Branch Junction. The loco, a class mourned since its demise from BR in 1988, has been freshly painted by the enthusiastic staff at Tinsley depot who have also applied replica wooden nameplates to the engine. 45104 was the original D59, Derby-built and new to traffic during February 1962. It was withdrawn in the week commencing 23rd April 1988, ten months after this picture was taken. At the time of writing it still languishes in Tinsley Secondary Yard along with other members of its class. The picture shows the loco about to be coupled onto a rake of Civil Engineer's wagons bound for Edge Hill, Liverpool.

CENTRE LEFT: 47446, in revised blue livery with large BR logos, and part of Tinsley's Railfreight Distribution fleet, FDCT, stands in the Wimpey Waste Disposal Terminal, Appley Bridge, which is situated by the ex-Lancashire and Yorkshire line between Wigan Wallgate and Southport. It is just about to leave light engine after bringing in the 6F60 MSx from Northenden, a working nicknamed locally the 'binliner train'. The whole formation will have firstly travelled forward as far as Burscough Bridge Station where run-round facilities are located, enabling the train to be propelled into the exchange sidings at the Wimpey Terminal. The containers from the train are just being unloaded and the whole operation takes several hours, hence the loco's return to Springs Branch depot, Wigan, where it will lay over for three hours before returning to Appley Bridge. The landfill site located in the West Quarry at Appley Bridge was closed during February 1991 and all workings have been transferred to a new facility at Parbold three miles west of Appley Bridge. This new terminal will receive three trains per day from Northenden and Dean Lane. The Pacer unit is working the 12.32 ex-Manchester Victoria to Southport local train.

LOWER LEFT: 20140 and 20157, both in original BR 'weatherstained' blue livery, are pictured passing Abram Opencast coal site, propelling the 7T75 from Bickershaw Colliery to Fiddlers Ferry Power Station. Unfortunately the Abram site, unlike Bickershaw, despatches all its coal by road. Hauling the 7T75, and out of picture, are 20195 and 20159, all locos being members of the FEGN pool based at Toton; 20157 however has now been withdrawn. 20195 and 20159 will be detached at Springs Branch Junction and 20140 along with 20157 will become the train engines for the southerly journey down the WCML to Warrington Arpley yard. Two pairs of Class 20s are used on the three mile branch to Bickershaw so that a 'top and tail' situation can take place, there being no run round facilities at the colliery. The pairs of 20s perform well with 45 HAAs up the steep 1 in 60 gradient which is encountered from Platt Bridge. A token is received at the former site of Platt Bridge Station which is unusual as the branch is worked as a 'one train in section' line. From October 1991 the plan is to replace the 40 or so FEGN pool of Class 20s with just twelve Class 60s which will be allocated to Toton depot like the Class 20s but will be outstabled at Springs Branch depot where A and B exams will take place. Two Class 60s, 60015 and 60016, arrived at Springs Branch for crew training in January 1991, so the writing is now on the wall for the ever-popular English Electric Class 20s. Bickershaw Colliery lies on a spur off the now-lifted ex-LNWR line between Wigan and Manchester via Tyldesley. The rusting rails to the left of the picture were originally a through double-tracked route between Wigan and Kenyon Junction where the main Liverpool to Manchester line was joined. However this route is now truncated at Bickershaw.

RIGHT: 20158, now sadly withdrawn, is pictured in happier days with sister loco 20168 propelling 45 HAA hoppers at ½ mph under the rapid loader at Bickershaw Colliery, both locos being part of the Toton FEGN fleet. The working will depart to Fiddlers Ferry as the 7T77 and will convey 1,000 tonnes of coal. Bickershaw Colliery complex includes Golborne and Parsonage pits which are linked underground. All the coal extracted is conveyed to Bickershaw where it is graded and washed before loading into HAA hoppers. The loading operations are carefully carried out by the private firm of Lindley Plant Ltd who are based in Derbyshire and have recently won the contract from British Coal to carry out this delicate operation. Fiddlers Ferry receives up to 100,000 tonnes of coal each week all by the MGR system. By 1990, Bickershaw and Parkside had become the only two pits in Lancashire which are still rail-served, and during a 24-hour period can despatch six loaded trains to Fiddlers Ferry. Workings from Yorkshire are greatly reduced since the beginning of the 1980s when the Woodhead line was closed and lifted. Today two MGR trains per day cross the Pennines from Yorkshire, originating from Doncaster Decoy Yard which replaced Healey Mills as a coal-staging yard in 1989. Staffordshire has become a second choice behind Lancashire to sent MGR traffic to Fiddlers Ferry, Silverdale Colliery, near Stoke, despatching up to four workings a day.

BELOW: The location is Fiddlers Ferry Power Station, and 20081 and 20045, again both in BR standard blue livery and members of the FEGN loco pool are ready to leave the exchange siding, after receiving the signal that the road ahead is clear for the journey back to Bickershaw with the 7T76 working. 20045 has recently been withdrawn. They will follow the usual procedure at Warrington Arpley of being dragged by an 08 shunter into Arpley Yard so that they can proceed northwards up the WCML to Springs Branch Junction and then Bickershaw. At Wigan another pair of Class 20s will be attached for the run up the branch to the colliery. Fiddlers Ferry opened in 1969 when there was a growing demand for electricity, and today has capacity to produce 2000 mega watts. Because the Power Station accepts MGR trains from Yorkshire and Staffordshire as well as from the local pits, two lines were constructed through the discharge hopper house to accommodate two loads at the same time. However, in practice one train load uses the facility which takes about 80 minutes for 45 HAA hoppers to discharge its coal.

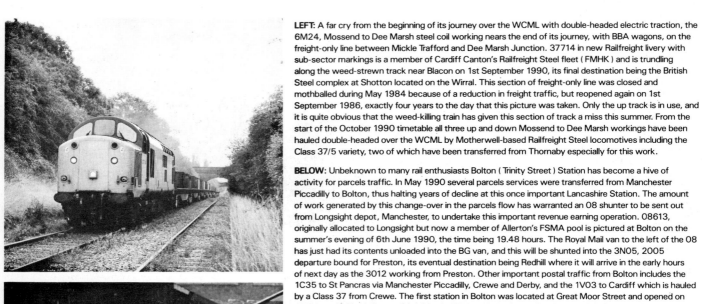

LEFT: A far cry from the beginning of its journey over the WCML with double-headed electric traction, the 6M24, Mossend to Dee Marsh steel coil working nears the end of its journey, with BBA wagons, on the freight-only line between Mickle Trafford and Dee Marsh Junction. 37714 in new Railfreight livery with sub-sector markings is a member of Cardiff Canton's Railfreight Steel fleet (FMHK) and is trundling along the weed-strewn track near Blacon on 1st September 1990, its final destination being the British Steel complex at Shotton located on the Wirral. This section of freight-only line was closed and mothballed during May 1984 because of a reduction in freight traffic, but reopened again on 1st September 1986, exactly four years to the day that this picture was taken. Only the up track is in use, and it is quite obvious that the weed-killing train has given this section of track a miss this summer. From the start of the October 1990 timetable all three up and down Mossend to Dee Marsh workings have been hauled double-headed over the WCML by Motherwell-based Railfreight Steel locomotives including the Class 37/5 variety, two of which have been transferred from Thornaby especially for this work.

BELOW: Unbeknown to many rail enthusiasts Bolton (Trinity Street) Station has become a hive of activity for parcels traffic. In May 1990 several parcels services were transferred from Manchester Piccadilly to Bolton, thus halting years of decline at this once important Lancashire Station. The amount of work generated by this change-over in the parcels flow has warranted an 08 shunter to be sent out from Longsight depot, Manchester, to undertake this important revenue earning operation. 08613, originally allocated to Longsight but now a member of Allerton's FSMA pool is pictured at Bolton on the summer's evening of 6th June 1990, the time being 19.48 hours. The Royal Mail van to the left of the 08 has just had its contents unloaded into the BG van, and this will be shunted into the 3N05, 2005 departure bound for Preston, its eventual destination being Redhill where it will arrive in the early hours of next day as the 3O12 working from Preston. Other important postal traffic from Bolton includes the 1C35 to St Pancras via Manchester Piccadilly, Crewe and Derby, and the 1V03 to Cardiff which is hauled by a Class 37 from Crewe. The first station in Bolton was located at Great Moor Street and opened on 11th June 1831, closing on 29th March 1954, and now becoming the site of the inevitable car park. Trinity Street Station, now known in the BR timetable as just Bolton, was opened on 29th May 1838 and occupied part of the Great Moor Street site. A £3 million modernisation scheme began at Bolton Station in 1986, and the ex-Lancashire and Yorkshire station now forms part of a bus/rail interchange.

LEFT: The time is 03.45 on 26th October 1988 and 08423, now sadly withdrawn, is pictured under the lights of Warrington Arpley Speedlink yard at the head of three PCA tanks which will depart at 07.30 as the 6N73 Sx working to Blackburn. The PCAs will then be tripped onto the Ribblesdale Cement Works located to the north of Clitheroe on the freight-only line between Blackburn and Hellifield, access to the works being via Horrocksford Junction. The oil tanks pictured left will leave the yard at 05.45 as the Arpley to Ellesmere Port oil empties. The Speedlink yards at Warrington include both Arpley and Walton Old Junction. Arpley deals mainly with 'up' traffic and the smaller Walton Old Junction yard handles 'down' freight. Warrington is a very important Speedlink Yard located on the WCML and can deal with over 100 workings per day. This figure does not include the local Fiddlers Ferry Power Station to Bickershaw MGR coal traffic which brings an additional four workings each way through the yard five days a week with two trains on a Saturday morning. With the announcement in December 1990 of the impending closure of the Speedlink Network from July 1991, traffic utilising Warrington could be greatly reduced.

BELOW: One of the highlights for enthusiasts on the evening of 19th July 1989 must have been the sight of two Class 26 locomotives, 26008 along with sister engine 26007 powering north through Warrington Bank Quay station at the head of a train consisting of long-welded rail. Both locos in Railfreight Coal livery are allocated to Eastfield depot and are part of the Power Station Coal Scottish fleet (FEPE) although now 26008 is a member of the Scottish Civil Engineer's DCHA pool. This picture truly was a case of BR motive power...Off the beaten track. The locos had arrived earlier in the day on a Mossend to Dee Marsh steel coil train, unusual in itself. The reason for this exclusive Scottish class to be found so far south of the border was the one-day rail strikes which had been called at the time by both ASLEF and the NUR. However by 27th July both unions had settled their differences with BR, and it is highly unlikely that this class of loco will be seen as far south again, unless of course they are on their way to Vic Berry's yard at Leicester for cutting!

LEFT: With the Partington Shell oil refinery and chemical works forming the backdrop, 47118, a Tinsley-based Railfreight Distribution loco (FDBT, overdue an F exam), is about to leave the industrial complex with its load of TCA Styrene tanks bound for Baglan Bay in South Wales. It will run as the 6V71 Tuo from Partington (Shell). Since 3rd December 1990, 47118, has been in store at Tinsley. It was officially condemned on 1st March 1991 and was notable by the fact that between December 1965 and November 1970 it ran as a Class 48! 47118 had arrived light engine from Crewe and would be worked back as far as Hereford on the South and West route by the Crewe driver, secondman and guard. This working usually conveys twelve TCA tanks as can be seen by the numbered discharge gantries but on this occasion, 17th September 1990, an extra two TCAs had been added due to an increase in production at the Shell plant. The freight-only branch from Partington to Skelton Junction also services the ICI Carrington Power Station complex but at the time of writing the only regular traffic was to and from the Shell oil refinery. The ex-CLC branch originally continued from Skelton Junction over the Manchester Ship Canal and linked up with the Manchester Central to Warrington Central line at Glazebrook East Junction. The line is now truncated by the Manchester Ship Canal bridge.

LEFT: 47380, *Immingham*, pictured in the original Railfreight livery and based in the Petroleum Pool at Immingham depot (FPCI), propels its load of 100 tonne oil tanks into the private sidings of British Tar Products based at Glazebrook after arriving as the 02.15, 6M18 Tho from Lindsey Oil Refinery, the date being 13th May 1988. Note the loco has non-standard oval buffers. This short freight-only branch leaves the ex-Cheshire Lines Committee main Manchester to Warrington Central route at Glazebrook East Junction. The British Tar plant can receive up to three workings per day both from Immingham and Haverton Hill on Teeside. There is also the 6V65 return empties which leaves Glazebrook for Waterston in South Wales on Mondays only. The locos on these workings return light engine to Longsight Depot, Manchester, for servicing, returning later in the day to pick up the empties. The lattice-girdered bridge seen to the right above the third oil tanker used to carry the ex-CLC line between Partington Junction and Glazebrook East Junction but was taken out of use on 3rd August 1982. By this time the route was barely used and had been singled at the beginning of the 1970s. Closure avoided expensive repairs to the bridge which spans the Manchester Ship Canal at this point.

UPPER LEFT: Under a threatening sky, 47324 *Glossidae* is waiting to propel its train of empty TEA tanks out of Ravenhead sidings, St. Helens, after arriving on the 6F53 from Stanlow. A complicated traffic movement now takes place on the Stanlow workings as there are no run-round facilities at Pilkingtons' Cowley Hill Works, which are also served by the 6F53. Trains used to arrive at Ravenhead and Cowley Hill via St. Helens Junction but this line was disconnected during January 1990, workings now having to travel via St. Helens Central, a far more circuitous route from Stanlow and Warrington. Trains arrive at St. Helens Central Station via the WCML, Bamfurlong Junction and Ince Moss Junction. At St. Helens the TEA tanks are propelled into Cowley Hill Works and after discharging its oil from five tanks the train will continue through St. Helens Central station on to the truncated freight-only route to Ravenhead sidings for the remaining five TEAs to be emptied. The loco is able to run round here, propel out from Ravenhead in order to gain access to Central Station, and eventually the WCML and southwards to Warrington. Just think how much quicker and simpler this operation would be if the St. Helens Junction line had not been disconnected.

CENTRE LEFT: On a bright winter's afternoon the driver of 47194 *Bullidae* has just opened up the regulator for the final approach to Ravenhead Sidings, St. Helens, which lie to the left of this picture. 47194 belongs to Crewe's FPBC fleet and is working the 6F53 MTTho, which contains ten TEA oil tanks from Stanlow. It will propel its train into the works sidings where the loco can run round. Five tanks will already have been emptied at Pilkingtons' Cowley Hill site; just the remaining five are discharged at Ravenhead. The Ravenhead site also receives a twice-weekly working from Robeston in South Wales which runs on a Wednesday and Friday as the 6M51. Recently this train has been hauled by a pair of Cardiff Canton's Class 37s from the FPEK Petroleum Pool. The line in the foreground used to run through to St Helens Junction as a freight-only route but is now truncated at the Hayes Chemical Sidings. All signals and trackwork in this area were rationalised during 1990 and duties are worked as simple 'one train in section'.

ST. HELENS

LOWER LEFT: The shunter of the 6F58 which runs on a MTTho is communicating with St. Helen's signalbox on a two-way radio in order to allow the Ravenhead to Stanlow return oil empties to regain access to the main line at St. Helens Central Station. 47324 *Glossidae*, a Crewe Railfreight Petroleum engine (FPBC), had ten TEAs in tow and is waiting on the remains of the freight-only line between St. Helens Central and St. Helens Junction stations. Ravenhead signalbox and its associated signalling were taken out of use in July 1990, and now 'one train working' is used when a delivery of oil is made to Ravenhead. The line to the junction is now truncated at Hayes Chemical Sidings which itself receives one trip a day from Warrington Arpley yard. The sidings to Ravenhead, rail-connected since 1849, are immediately in front of 47324, curving away to the right of the picture.

FACING PAGE: 37680 in the old Railfreight livery which included a pleasant-to-the-eye red solebar is pictured with sister loco 37688 *Great Rocks* in the new Railfreight livery of two-tone grey with sub-sector markings showing that it belongs to Tinsley's Railfreight Aggregates Pool (FABT). They are pictured approaching Navigation Road, Altrincham, with the 7F50, 15.29 ex-Tunstead to Oakleigh limestone working on Sunday, 23rd September 1990. The picture is taken from an overbridge on the ex-LNWR Skelton Junction to Warrington Arpley freight-only line which unfortunately was taken out of use on 7th July 1985. By this time the eleven mile route was host to just 20 odd freights a day compared with over 60 in 1979. The overbridge in the background carries chemical traffic from Baglan Bay in South Wales to the Shell complex at Partington, where the line is now truncated. It used to be a through CLC freight route between Skelton Junction and Glazebrook East Junction but the line was taken out of use on 3rd August 1982, having already been singled. On the 15th May 1989 as part of the new Network North-West launch the freight-only line between Skelton Junction, Northenden, and Stockport was re-opened for Chester to Manchester Oxford Road passenger trains in order to remove them from the busy section of line between Deansgate Junction and Cornbrook Junction. This also enabled the service to serve Stockport for the first time.

UPPER RIGHT: ICI Winnington's GEC-built Ludwig Mond 0-6-0 shunter is pictured on 17th August 1990 entering the BR exchange sidings at Oakleigh near Northwich with a rake of TEA tanks bound for Ellesmere Port. ICI Winnington also operate an ex-BR 08 shunter and has its own diesel maintenance shed. The line of PCA tanks in the background contain soda ash and are destined for Rockware Glass at Barnby Dun, near Doncaster. The exchange sidings at Oakleigh are due to be rationalised early in 1991 to make for better shunting paths within the yard. Traffic however is buoyant and along with the Tunstead to Oakleigh crushed limestone workings which operate seven days a week, the yard can accommodate up to three coal workings per week from the Stoke area.

CENTRE RIGHT: Running 1½ hours early, quite usual for freight traffic, 47971 *Robin Hood*, is quite unusual as choice of motive power, being a Departmental Research Railway Technical Centre loco (DRTC) at the head of the 6M27 So from Larbert to Oakleigh empty soda ash train which is actually sponsored by the Chemical arm of BR Railfreight!. The reason for this was the failure of the booked Cardiff Class 37 at Warrington Arpley Stabling Point, the 47 being the only available substitute power. The 18 PCA tanks will have left Larbert at 06.15 and power over the WCML will have been a pair of Class 86/6 electrics, diesel power being attached at Warrington for the run to

Oakleigh via Hartford LNW Junction, Hartford CLC Junction and then Greenbank South Junction which gives access to the freight-only Oakleigh line.

RIGHT: 37885, a member of Cardiff Canton's Railfreight Steel fleet (FMHK) is pictured leaving Oakleigh BR exchange sidings, Northwich, to return light engine to Warrington Arpley Yard, the date being 18th August 1990. It had arrived with the PCA tanks pictured centre and was running as the 6M27 So Larbert to Oakleigh. 37885 would have replaced two AC electric locomotives at Arpley Yard and itself would have arrived in Warrington with an earlier Cardiff to Dee Marsh metals working. It is common practice for Arpley TOPS office to use Cardiff Class 37s on such workings at the weekend rather than have the loco stand idle on Arpley Stabling Point.

ABOVE: 47446 in BR revised blue livery with large logos is pictured passing the ex-CLC station at Plumley with the 7H52 Oakleigh to Tunstead empty ICI limestone working on 10th July 1990. The ICI quarry at Tunstead in the Peak District is served mainly by the BR Railfreight Construction sub-sector but the Tunstead to Oakleigh traffic is handled by Railfreight Distribution hence the use of 47446 which is allocated to the Crewe Distribution loco fleet (FDCC). 47446 is presently allocated to Tinsley and is part of the FDBT pool. This pool of 37 locos will all be condemned in July 1991 when Railfreight Distribution will rationalise and reorganise its Class 47 fleet upon closure of the Speedlink network. The PHV hoppers behind the loco are unusual because they are vacuum-braked and have been in use on this traffic since 1937, making them 53 years old! Currently the limestone flow between Tunstead and Oakleigh runs three times a day, seven days a week. The PHV fleet numbers about 150 vehicles and has caused something of a problem for ICI, who own the wagons. The reason is that Class 60 locos are due to be introduced on to the workings during 1991 but these engines have no facilities for operating vacuum brakes. A short term solution is to retain a small fleet of vacuum-fitted Class 37s to operate alongside the Class 60s, the 37s being used on short haul workings.

FACING PAGE: On a beautiful summer's morning, 30th June 1988, 37127 and 37160 are pictured passing the grounds of Hoghton Tower on the East Lancashire line between Blackburn and Preston with the 6S83 Clitheroe (Ribblesdale Cement Works) to Gunnie (Castle Cement works) conveying PCA tanks. Since this picture was taken 37127 has been renumbered to 37370 but remains in the Motherwell Railfreight Aggregates Pool (FACM) whilst 37160 became 37373 and remains in the same sector as 37370. Both these locos were regular performers on this duty during 1990. The 6S83 runs on a Monday-to-Friday basis and along with the 6F84 Blackburn to Warrington Speedlink trip, and the 6G32 Blackburn to Washwood Heath, is the only freight traffic to traverse the East Lancashire line. During March 1989, however, steel coil traffic in the form of the 6M25 Mossend to Dee Marsh travelled the route with Class 20s as motive power when the WCML was closed at Tebay due to engineering work. 37370/373 are now in the Motherwell FALY pool.

ABOVE: Drifting down the 1 in 80 from Copy Pit summit towards Kitson Wood Tunnel over the scenic Trans-Pennine crossing between Burnley (Manchester Road) and Todmorden is 37054 in ex-works condition, and a member of Thornaby's Railfreight Steel pool of locos (FMTY). The train is running as the 6Z81 special from Walkers of Lower Darwen, Blackburn, conveying empty steel-covered continental wagons bound for Lackenby on Teeside. This line was constructed by the Lancashire and Yorkshire Railway Company and opened on 12th November 1849, however the route was nearly abandoned by BR when a large landslip occurred on 13th October 1986. After months of uncertainty the line was reopened and a 'Roses Link' was formed in 1987 connecting Blackpool with York mainly on the initiative of the Burnley Building Society which merged with the Bradford based Provincial Building Society, forming the National and Provincial. A reliable form of transport was needed between the two head offices to convey its workers, roads in this area of the Pennines often being blocked with snow in the winter months. Today freight traffic is rare but on odd occasions the Lindsey Oil Refinery (Immingham) to Preston Dock traffic is routed this way.

BELOW: Standing at the private sidings of the Metal Box Company in Westhoughton is 37883, a Cardiff-based Railfreight Steel loco (FMHK) with the 6H65 working bound for Trafford Park, Manchester. Tin plate is being unloaded from SHA and SPA wagons which have originated from the British Steel Corporation works located at Trostre in South Wales. The trip from Trostre has been a complicated one in order to reach Westhoughton, the train diagram being as follows:-

6B16	Trostre BS Tin Plate Works to Margam via Llanelli	6B78 Margam to Cardiff Tidal Si
6M46	Cardiff Tidal Sidings to Trafford Park	6F65 Trafford Park to Westhoug

a journey via the South and West route which takes over sixteen hours. Until October 1989 Metal Box was served by Railfreight Distribution on a Warrington Arpley-Westhoughton-Chorley-Warrington Arpley Speedlink diagram. This service, however, was withdrawn but the steel traffic continued and runs once a week as traffic demands. The working can be very unpredictable, sometimes running as often as four times a week and usually up to two hours early!

UPPER LEFT: Passing along the rubbish-strewn track of the Deepdale branch, Preston, is 37217, a member of Cardiff Canton's Railfreight Coal Distribution fleet of locos (FQCK). It still retains its original rail blue livery. 37217 is working the 6N48 Washwood Heath to Deepdale Coal Concentration Depot conveying phurnacite in HEA hoppers from South Wales pits for household use in the Lancashire area. The branch which originally ran to Longridge was built to convey stone from Longridge Fells to Preston Docks. It lost its passenger service as long ago as 1930 but freight traffic continued to serve Longridge until 1967. The coal depot lies on the site of the original Preston and Longridge railway terminus in Deepdale Street. A reversal has to take place at Deepdale Junction where only a shunting neck remains towards Longridge; this follows closure in 1980 of Courtaulds Red Scar factory which was located ½ mile south of Grimsargh. Today the Deepdale branch is host to two trains from Washwood Heath, running on a Tuesday and Thursday only.

CENTRE LEFT: 37212 passes through the unstaffed station at Bamber Bridge on the Preston to Blackburn line with the 6G32 Tho Preston Deepdale to Washwood Heath working conveying HEA hoppers carrying domestic coal which has originated from Pantyffynnon in South Wales. 37212 in the new Railfreight livery with sub-sector markings is a member of Cardiff Canton's Railfreight Coal Distribution loco fleet (FQCK) and has already traversed the Deepdale branch to service the National Fuels depot. British Fuels, King Street, Blackburn, is 37212s next booked stop, but on this particular day 37212 had been stopped at Bamber Bridge to propel its train into the Civil Engineer's sidings where a 'cripple' HEA hopper had been removed from the train before the final run to Blackburn could commence. However the formation was still running 80 minutes early at this point!

RIGHT: 47449, a member of Crewe's Railfreight Distribution fleet (FDCC), but now in Tinsley's FDBT pool, is pictured passing the unusually designed Lancashire and Yorkshire signalbox at Bamber Bridge with the 6F84 Blackburn to Warrington Arpley Speedlink trip working on the misty morning of 29th November 1990. It is conveying traffic from Fogarty's Distribution Company's works based in Blackburn, the continental cargo wagon at the rear of the train having been attached at the premises of W. H. Bowker on the inward journey to Blackburn. It contains empty chemical drums returning to West Germany. In August 1990, with the aid of a Section 8 government grant, a new road/rail terminal was opened at Bowker's six-acre site at Bamber Bridge which is adjacent to the East Lancashire rail corridor. The terminal offers warehouse facilities and undercover loading for cargo wagons. Within two years the company hope to handle 50,000 tonnes of rail-borne traffic, keeping heavy lorries off our already choked road system.

LEFT: Immingham's 47379 *Total Energy* displaying new Railfreight livery belonging to the Petroleum Pool (FPCI) pierces the early morning mist at 06.46 as it approaches the ICI Hillhouses complex located at Burn Naze on the truncated Fleetwood branch which closed to passenger traffic on 1st June 1970. The 6M45 working is conveying empty VCM tanks (Vinyl chloride monomer) from Barry in South Wales. Over the last eighteen months the signalbox at Thornton has been demolished and an automatic barrier now controls the road crossing. Signalling on the route has also been simplified and is controlled from the box at Poulton le Fylde where the Fleetwood branch joins the main Preston to Blackpool line.

RIGHT: 47605 in the new Railfreight livery of two-tone grey but minus its sub-sector markings is pictured passing the overgrown station platforms at Burn Naze Halt on the 6V26 VCM working from the ICI Hillhouses complex to Barry Docks. 47605 was a member of the Crewe FDCC Railfreight Distribution fleet when this picture was taken on 15th July 1990 but has since joined Tinsley's FDCT pool, and is due to be stored from July 1991. The Preston and Wyre Railway from Preston to Fleetwood was opened on 15th July 1840 with 20,000 passengers carried in the first month. The Preston and Wyre was taken over jointly by the L & Y and LNWR on 28th July 1849, but it wasn't until 1892 that Fleetwood became the largest fishing port on the West Coast, all the fish traffic being despatched by rail. Burn Naze Halt was opened on 1st February 1909, and before closure came in 1970 was used by workers from ICI Hillhouses plant which can be seen behind 47605. The line between Burn Naze and the terminus at Fleetwood and Wyre Dock was closed on 18th April 1966 and has now been lifted. Burn Naze chemical traffic is the only reason the line survives today!

LOWER FACING: Crewe Diesel's Railfreight Distribution loco, FDCC, 47594, but now a member of Bristol's RXLD fleet has just arrived light engine at Burn Naze, ICI Hillhouses complex, from Springs Branch depot, Wigan, on the summer evening of 22nd July 1990. It has been coupled by the travelling BR shunter to six loaded VCM tanks and will now draw forward to collect the six VCMs in the adjacent siding. 47594 will then convey the twelve tanks from the ICI complex on to the remains of the Fleetwood branch before running round its train for the return journey to Barry in South Wales as the 6V26 Suo working. The Springs Branch crew will take the working as far as Wigan where Crewe men will take it over to Hereford. The Fleetwood branch sees four workings a week from Barry, including the 6V26, which is usually worked by a Cardiff Petroleum FPEK based loco, not a Distribution engine!

BURN NAZE

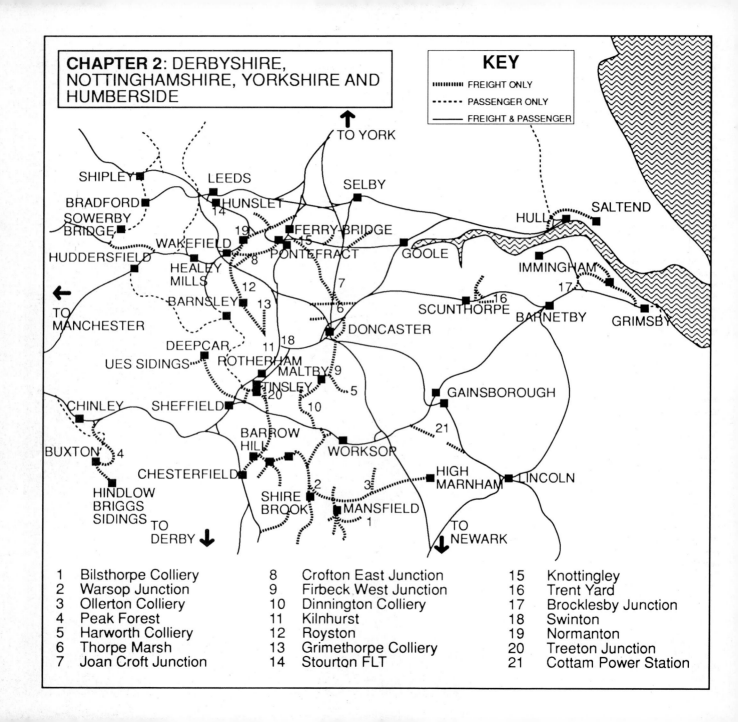

CHAPTER 2: DERBYSHIRE, NOTTINGHAMSHIRE, YORKSHIRE AND HUMBERSIDE

KEY

|||||||| FREIGHT ONLY

- - - - PASSENGER ONLY

——— FREIGHT & PASSENGER

TO YORK

SHIPLEY
LEEDS
SELBY
BRADFORD
HUNSLET
14
SALTEND
SOWERBY
BRIDGE
19
FERRY BRIDGE
HULL
WAKEFIELD
15
PONTEFRACT
GOOLE
HUDDERSFIELD
8
IMMINGHAM
HEALEY
MILLS
7
12
SCUNTHORPE
17
BARNSLEY
13
6
BARNETBY
TO
MANCHESTER
GRIMSBY
18
DONCASTER
DEEPCAR
11
UES SIDINGS
ROTHERHAM
MALTBY
9
GAINSBOROUGH
TINSLEY
20
5
CHINLEY
SHEFFIELD
10
21
BARROW
HILL
WORKSOP
BUXTON
4
HIGH
LINCOLN
CHESTERFIELD
MARNHAM
HINDLOW
2
3
BRIGGS
SIDINGS
SHIRE
BROOK
MANSFIELD
TO
DERBY
1
TO
NEWARK

1	Bilsthorpe Colliery	8	Crofton East Junction	15	Knottingley
2	Warsop Junction	9	Firbeck West Junction	16	Trent Yard
3	Ollerton Colliery	10	Dinnington Colliery	17	Brocklesby Junction
4	Peak Forest	11	Kilnhurst	18	Swinton
5	Harworth Colliery	12	Royston	19	Normanton
6	Thorpe Marsh	13	Grimethorpe Colliery	20	Treeton Junction
7	Joan Croft Junction	14	Stourton FLT	21	Cottam Power Station

UPPER RIGHT: A picture which truly illustrates why BR are so committed to limestone traffic in the Peak District.... 37681 with sister loco 37414, an ex-Plymouth Laira engine, but now a member of Tinsley's Railfreight Aggregates Pool (FABT), is seen approaching Dove Holes Tunnel, 1 mile 1224 yards long, through a deep imposing limestone cutting, a feature synonymous with this section of freight-only line close to Peak Forest Yard. 37681 and 37414 are both in new Railfreight livery with construction sub-sector markings and are now both members of Immingham's FABI pool. They are working the 6M42 from Dove Holes RMC (Ready Mixed Concrete) Quarry to Washwood Heath conveying a full load of 23 JGA 90 tonne hoppers of roadstone. The formation is being banked at the rear by 37686 because of the steep gradient to Dove Holes Tunnel. This line was once the Midland Railways direct route to London from Manchester but local passenger traffic had disappeared by March 1967, and express workings followed in July 1968. However the Peak Forest area still keeps its links with the past; the local pub is still called the Midland Hotel. Dove Holes tunnel, the longest on the Manchester to St Pancras former Midland route caused problems in its construction from day one for its Victorian railway engineers. They discovered an underground river which had to be diverted at much extra cost. The tunnel collapsed in 1872 just five years after it had opened. It did so again in 1940 and by 1954 night time workings through the tunnel had been banned due to its unsound condition. In fact the poor condition of the tunnel was one of the reasons which BR put forward for closing the line as a through passenger route to St Pancras. Today the tunnel has a speed restriction imposed upon it but still sees a great deal of stone traffic passing through each day and night!

LOWER RIGHT: In a desolate and isolated part of the BR freight network, 47439, a Crewe diesel Railfreight Distribution engine in revised blue livery is pictured at Briggs Sidings, Hindlow. With the 6T82 trip to Peak Forest, sponsored by Railfreight Distribution, it will eventually feed into the 6F17 to Warrington Arpley Yard later in the day. This working is certainly going to be a casualty of the Speedlink Network closure which is scheduled for July. The 6T82 can also be tripped to Earles Sidings at Hope and BR's Buxton MPD conveying cement and oil respectively. 47439 now based at Immingham in the FABI pool is attached to just one PBA tank of limestone from the Steetley Plant at Briggs Sidings which is bound for Rockware Glass at Kirk Sandall near Doncaster. Briggs Sidings can boast an altitude of 1267ft. above sea level, considerably higher than the famous Shap summit on the WCML which stands at 1169ft. above sea level. In the days of passenger traffic the line between Buxton and Ashbourne was regularly blocked with snow! The most profitable part of the 6T82 trip working is the Earles Sidings at Hope to Northenden cement traffic which is run by Railfreight Construction. As long as this work remains buoyant the Construction sector is willing to allow the Railfreight Distribution limestone traffic to be attached at Hindlow, therefore the Steetley traffic may survive after 8th July 1991, when the Speedlink Network is due to close.

ABOVE: 37686 in Tinsley's FABT pool and sporting the old Railfreight style of livery draws the 6M42 out of the RMC (Ready Mixed Concrete) Dove Holes quarry located just north of Peak Forest, its consignment of roadstone being bound for Washwood Heath, Birmingham. 37686 now an Immingham FABI pool loco will eventually become the banker for this train because of the steep gradients within the Peak Forest area. A brace of Class 37s will be the train locos. Peak Forest can see up to seven departures daily to places all over Britain and including Ely, Hope Street (Salford), Leeds (Balm Road), Selby and Bletchley. In August 1990 a special 6Z39 working ran from Peak Forest to Worcester conveying 22 PSA vehicles. This 'on trial' traffic has a possibility of further runs when a newly constructed stone plant is installed at Worcester. The Ely traffic handles limestone used in the sugar making process and these workings are run seasonally between October and January, but RMC have just lost this contract to road haulage contractors. However all is not doom and gloom at RMC because during 1991 the quarry at Dove Holes is hoping to introduce a new flow of roadstone traffic to Ely North Junction which will run 'all year round'. Note the newly acquired RMC shunter in the foreground which will be more generally used when the roadstone traffic to Ely comes on flow.

RIGHT: 37678 and 37681, now members of Immingham's FABI Construction pool, are completely dwarfed by the limestone crushing plant at ICI Hindlow, located on the ex-Buxton to Ashbourne line which was authorised in 1874, opened to goods in 1892 and to passengers in 1899, but lost its passenger service in November 1954 after 55 years loyal service. The 7T81 trip from ICI Tunstead, Britain's largest limestone quarry, to Hindlow conveying 17 ICI-owned PHV hoppers carrying 1200 tonnes is a relatively new Railfreight Construction Sub-sector working. In 1986 ICI decided to cease quarrying at Hindlow and this eventually led in January 1989 to the running of two daily services from ICI Tunstead. These operate seven days a week except on Christmas Day and Boxing Day, with limestone for the crushing plant. The finished product unfortunately is transported away by road to various water treatment and chemical plants throughout Great Britain, a great loss to Railfreight Construction.

LEFT: High on a limestone ledge at Warsop Junction are 20059 in old Railfreight livery comprising grey sides, yellow cabs, red buffer beams and the full height BR logo, and 20085 in Standard rail blue. They are both members of the Toton Power Station Coal Nottingham fleet, FEFN. The line in the foreground is the ex-Midland Railway route between Barrow Hill and Pye Bridge Junction which lies just south of Alfreton and Mansfield Parkway Station. The locos are shunting the private yard and sidings of WH Davis's Wagon Works which repair all types of tankers and wagons for BR and the private owner fleet. Some PCA tanks can just be seen behind the Class 20s.

ABOVE: A delightful rural railway scene which could have been taken over 30 years ago. In fact it was taken on 19th July 1990 and shows Class 20s, 20080 and 20023, members of Toton's FEGN North West coal fleet, on loan to the Nottinghamshire Power Station coal pool at the time. They are waiting for signals to come off the private siding branch from WH Davis's Wagon Repair Works. The 20s have two PFAs in tow and are bound for Derby having recently been repaired at the wagon works. The main line in the centre of the picture is ex-Midland and used heavily by MGR coal traffic running between Pye Bridge Junction and Worksop whilst the line to the right formed the connecting spur from the Midland line to the ex-Great Central route which ran between Chesterfield and Lincoln. This line survives today serving four collieries as well as High Marnham Power Station where the line is truncated. Tuxford BP oil-loading terminal is also en route but is serviced by BR on an irregular basis. The ex-Midland-designed Shirebrook Junction signalbox and the semaphore signalling still on wooden posts make this a delightful area for the period railway photographer'.

LEFT: British Rail's Doncaster-built 58019 *Shirebrook Colliery*, a member of Toton's Nottingham Power Station coal fleet, FEAN, is pictured running on ex-Great Central metals as it approaches Clipstone West Junction with the 7G38, HAA empties, from Avenue National Smokeless Fuels Depot located near Clay Cross, to Clipstone Colliery on 19th June 1990. Clipstone can also boast an east and south junction which form a triangle with the west junction. This section of freight-only line sees heavy usage by Railfreight Coal services as there are at least half a dozen rail-served collieries within a few square miles of Clipstone Junction. These include Warsop Main, Welbeck, Blidworth, Bilsthorpe, Thoresby and Ollerton. All send coal to either West Burton or Cottam Power Stations via Worksop Yard. Toton's Class 58s are outstabled at Worksop and Shirebrook for this heavy MGR coal traffic, but from December 1990 it was proposed to base all Class 58s at Worksop where new facilities are being constructed. Barrow Hill's motive power will also be based at Worksop and the last roundhouse on BR will close. A group has been set up to try and save the listed building constructed by the Midland Railway in 1870.

FACING PAGE: 58027 is pictured in a delightful setting where wild daisies are clinging to the attractive but rugged limestone cutting through which 58027 is approaching Warsop Junction with the 7F53, Ollerton Colliery to Cottam Power Station MGR working. The 58, running on a single line in this location, belongs to the Toton FEBN sector. The train has just passed over the Shirebrook to Warsop Main Colliery line which will be known to many enthusiasts as the section of track to the east of Shirebrook Depot where Class 58s are stabled during the weekend lay-over. This line originally ran through to the ex-Great Central line situated to the north of Shirebrook, and from here Sheffield was eventually reached. The bridge in the background carries an accommodation road to a farm.

FACING PAGE: Bearing eastwards at Warsop Junction just to the north of Shirebrook MPD, which itself was due to close in December 1990, is 58035 in the new Railfreight livery with coal sub-sector markings and a member of Toton's FEBN fleet, as are most locos which work the Shirebrook area. 58035 has just left the ex-Midland line which ran between Shireoaks and Pye Bridge Junction located on the main Sheffield to Leicester line and has joined ex-Great Central metals which originally ran between Chesterfield Central and Lincoln Central. Only the section between Warsop Junction and High Marnham Power Station survives for MGR coal traffic. 58035 is working the 6G32 West Burton Power Station to Welbeck Colliery HAA empties. At Welbeck Colliery Junction the 58 will propel its train of HAAs into the colliery yard, and then after loading will have to run round its train for the journey back to West Burton. The myriad of freight lines in the Shirebrook area have been saved from extinction because of the large amount of coal still extracted from local pits. The coal can easily be transported by rail to local power stations, keeping many heavy lorries off the country roads which abound in this area of Nottinghamshire. For the freight train photographer there is one drawback, 99% of the workings are Class 58 hauled with HAA hoppers. However life becomes worthwhile if a pair of Class 20s appear on an unscheduled working!

WARSOP JUNCTION

LEFT: It is pleasing to see Class 20s still active on coal duties both in Lancashire and Yorkshire. However, with the delivery of Class 60s during 1991, the 20s will soon be withdrawn and yet another 'Modernisation Plan' diesel will have been lost. British Rail are hoping to withdraw all Class 20s by October 1991. In happier times, 20th June 1990, 20078 and 20151 both in very clean standard BR blue livery and members of the FEFN Toton coal fleet are pictured working the 7034 Oxcroft Colliery to Ridham Dock Paper Mill service which runs to the Southern Region location every weekday. A Class 56 will take over as motive power at Toton, the Class 20s having worked the train from Oxcroft because of the tight curvature of the colliery branch which is situated off the ex-Midland line between Barrow Hill and Shirebrook.

CENTRE LEFT: 58031 carrying coal sub-sector markings and a member of Toton's FEBN fleet is pictured with empty HAA hoppers on the 6G94 Ratcliffe Power Station to Warsop Junction Yard sidings, which are located just north of Shirebrook MPD. The HAAs will be stabled overnight and next day will form the 6G42 from Shirebrook Colliery, opened in 1896, to West Burton Power Station. The formation is travelling over former Midland metals and has just passed Hall Lane Junction where a single line spur links up with the ex-Midland main line at Foxlow Junction, situated to the north of Barrow Hill depot. The picture has been taken from an over-bridge, near Staveley, which used to carry the Great Central main line between Sheffield, Nottingham and London Marylebone, the Master Cutler being a famous express of the steam age using this once prestigious route. Unfortunately much of the Great Central, the last main line to be built in Britain, was closed and lifted in the early 1960s after the Beeching cuts, but the site of Staveley Great Central shed which was closed in 1965 can still be found to the south of Staveley Town Station, itself closing in May 1963. The pit head gear which can be seen in the top left of the picture is Artington Colliery, closed 60 years ago but today the headquarters of the local mines rescue service, being regularly used for training exercises.

BELOW: With Staveley Chemical Works forming the backdrop, 20190 and 20104, both members of the FEFN pool, Power Station Coal, Nottinghamshire locos based at Toton depot, are pictured approaching Barrow Hill Junction where access to the ex-Midland Main line between Chesterfield and Rotherham is gained. 20190 is in BR standard blue livery whilst 20104 is carrying old Railfreight livery which includes a red solebar. The locos are working the 7Z93 Ollerton Colliery to Ratcliffe Power Station and have 36 HAAs in tow. At Barrow Hill Railfreight Coal have numerous sidings which are used for staging HAA hoppers during the weekend lay-over, the sidings being located to the south of the depot. The line was double track in this area until the Spring of 1990 when the up line was lifted.

RIGHT: Fresh from Doncaster Works after an intermediate overhaul and repaint into Railfreight Distribution sub-sector colours, 37047 a member of Tinsley's FDET loco pool is about to propel the 6T02 out of the Rockware Glass factory sidings at Kirk Sandall to the north-east of Doncaster Station. The trip is bound for Belmont Railfreight Distribution Speedlink Yard. Nearby Decoy yard is a base for Trainload Coal and is so named because of wild duck shooting which was popular in the area before the arrival of the railway. The down yard at Decoy was opened in 1891, the up yard following four years later in 1895. The three PAAs behind 37047 will eventually join the 6M84 Doncaster to Warrington Railfreight Distribution service and will be tripped on from Arpley Yard to Oakleigh, BR's Exchange Sidings at Northwich which service ICI Winnington. Here the tanks will be loaded with soda ash, a chemical by-product, before returning to Rockware for use in the glass-making industry. The spillage on both tracks is from the sand train which runs each day from Middleton Towers, Kings Lynn, and services both the Rockware and Monk Bretton glass plants.

BELOW: On a beautiful summer's day, 21st June 1990, 58040 *Cottam Power Station*, a Toton FEBN pool engine, is running in the old Railfreight livery, light engine, past the Staveley Chemical Works en route to Shirebrook depot for servicing. The Staveley Chemical complex began life as the Staveley Coal and Iron Company. The railway first appeared in Staveley in 1840 but it was 51 years later in 1891 that the Iron Company could see the benefits of joining the rail network. The Company enjoyed a period in the enthusiasts' spotlight in the middle sixties when it employed two 'OF' steam engines built in 1907 by the Midland Railway Company. Designed by Deeley, 41528 and 41533, chosen mainly because of their short wheel base, worked the many miles of track within the Coal and Iron Works complex. Enthusiasts flocked to see them as other steam workings in the Barrow Hill and Staveley area had all but ceased. The locos were on hire from BR, and at weekends they would return to the nearby Staveley Midland shed (41E), also known as Barrow Hill to modern day enthusiasts. By 1888 the Midland lines had reached Clowne and Creswell, here joining Great Central metals. Two years later in 1890 a station was opened at Bolsover which could be reached via Seymour Junction. By 1930 Bolsover had lost its passenger traffic, Clowne following in 1954; however both towns are still rail-linked albeit on a MGR coal basis. Railfreight Coal serve at least eight pits along this now freight-only section of line.

ABOVE: The shunter of 58031 is about to pass the lamp off the 6G02, Harworth Colliery to Worksop Yard MGR train, to the driver after the loco had run round its trainload of HAA hoppers in the colliery yard. 58031, in new Railfreight livery with coal sub-sector markings, is allocated to Toton's FEBN pool. Harworth pit opened in 1924 and producing 1½ million tonnes per annum is situated on the freight-only ex-South Yorkshire Joint Railway system which came into being in 1909 after the amalgamation of five independent railway companies. Coal used to be dispatched from the colliery via the Great Northern branch which left the ECML just to the south of Scrooby. This line was closed in 1965 and has now been lifted. All coal traffic now leaves the pit on the South Yorkshire Joint System line via Firbeck West Junction which is located near the small village of Tickhill, the line being extended from Firbeck to Harworth in 1927. The line to the right of the HAA hoppers serves the Glass Bulb factory which receives a daily Speedlink trip working from Doncaster Belmont Yard.

LEFT: Toton's 58041 *Ratcliffe Power Station*, a member of the FEBN pool, Power Station Coal, Yorkshire, is pictured at Firbeck West Junction on the ex-South Yorkshire Joint Railway system which had been formed by the joining together of the Hull and Barnsley, Great Central, Great Northern, Lancashire & Yorkshire and the Dearne Valley Railway companies. 58041 is working the 6T93 from Doncaster Decoy Trainload Coal Yard to Maltby Colliery empties. The line to the right runs to Harworth Colliery and the Glass Bulb factory. Firbeck Junction was built as a triangle of lines with a north and east junction but today only the West Junction remains. From Maltby pit, opened in 1911 and producing one million tonnes per year, the train will work forward to Worksop Yard. Maltby receives and despatches four MGR coal trains per day.

LOWER FACING: Under a threatening sky the driver of 56014 is just about to receive the single line token from the signalman at Maltby Colliery South Box as he takes the 6G70 Worksop-Maltby Colliery-West Burton Power Station train forward into Maltby Colliery Yard. The South Yorkshire Joint System is still controlled by semaphore signalling and manual signal boxes which have been in use for well over 80 years, making locations along the route a railway photographer's paradise. Stations were originally opened at Tickhill and Wadworth, Maltby, and Dinnington with Laughton, but all had closed by 1929 when all passenger traffic ceased. 56014, a Toton FECN pool loco, is carrying the old Railfreight livery style but has recently been out-shopped from Doncaster Major Depot with new Railfreight colours and carrying coal sub-sector markings. The ex-South Yorkshire Joint line carries endless MGR coal trains during the week but at weekends the system is closed as the rail-served pits at Markham Main (Armthorpe), Harworth, Dinnington and Maltby run with reduced production.

LEFT: With the low winter's sun casting long shadows across the ex-South Yorkshire Joint Railway metals at Dinnington Colliery Junction, the driver of 37354 has just picked up the token for the single line section between Dinnington and Maltby Colliery South box. The Class 37, a Thornaby FALY Construction sub-sector loco, is pictured with two PAA British Industrial Sand (BIS) tanks in tow whilst working the 6T13 Doncaster Belmont to Worksop Speedlink trip on 16th March 1990. The PAAs contain sand from Middleton Towers, Kings Lynn, and are bound for the Co-op Glassworks located on a spur to the west of Worksop Yard. 37354 makes a pleasing sight and contrasts with the many Class 56s and 58s which monopolise MGR traffic on the ex-South Yorkshire Joint Railway System which runs between Kirk Sandall Junction to the north-east of Doncaster through to Dinnington. The line southwards from Dinnington to the main line at Brancliffe East Junction was originally constructed by the Midland and Great Central Joint Railway Committee.

UPPER LEFT: 47222, Appleby Frodingham, with non-standard oval buffers, and in original BR blue livery, is a member of Immingham's FPXA fleet which are stand-in locos awaiting the arrival of the Class 60 pool to Immingham depot, where training on Class 60s began in November 1990. The loco is working the 6E35 Leith to Immingham (Lindsey) oil empties and has just left the ECML on a spur from Joan Croft Junction located to the north of Doncaster. It has gained access to the freight-only line between Adwick Junction and Stainforth Junction at Applehurst Junction. The Joan Croft spur was opened on 1st July 1877, and 47222 is passing over ex-West Riding and Grimsby Railway metals. The bridge abutment which can just be seen above the seventh oil tank used to carry the Great Central and Hull & Barnsley Joint line which ran northwards from Thurcroft Colliery to the docks at Hull. The line was built in the early 1900s to transport coal from the then new South Yorkshire pits to Hull Docks for export. The line was closed and lifted in 1969 but is still walkable in places. The track on the left of the picture is an access line to Thorpe Marsh Power Station.

LOWER LEFT: With Thorpe Marsh Power Station prominent in the background a very clean Immingham-based 47369, until recently a member of the FPCI fleet but now transferred to the FPFR North Thames Petroleum pool, is pictured on the freight-only section of line between Stainforth Junction on the Doncaster to Hull main line and Adwick Junction on the Doncaster to Wakefield passenger route. 47369 is working the 6D71 Lindsey (Immingham) to Leeds oil tanks and will return later in the day, 13th July 1990, with the 6D34 return to Immingham. Thorpe Marsh Power Station is serviced regularly each weekday with MGR coal services emanating from pits in South Yorkshire. HAA hoppers are gathered in the exchange sidings at Worksop before onward movement to Thorpe Marsh.

THORPE MARSH

UPPER RIGHT: On a dull March day, 37066, still in BR Standard Blue Livery, is pictured just south of Treeton Junction on the ex-Midland freight-only line between Rotherham and Chesterfield. The Class 37, now running in Departmental grey livery and a member of Immingham's DCEA pool is working the 9E10 Bescot to Doncaster departmental service conveying flat BDA wagons loaded with sections of rail. The BDAs will be unloaded at Doncaster Wood Yard and the HEA coal hoppers which are 'hitching a ride' on this departmental working are destined for RFS Industries Wagon Works located to the west of Doncaster Station. Class 9 trains are restricted to 35mph and can either be fully or partially air braked. The section of track on the right used to provide access to the recently closed Orgreave Coking Plant.

CENTRE RIGHT: 37709 is just gaining access to the Doncaster Sheffield line as it leaves the Croda Hydrocarbons Work (Kilnhurst) located just south of the new Swinton Station. 37709, an Immingham Petroleum North Thames pool engine, FPFR, in new Railfreight livery with Petroleum sub-sector markings, is working the 6L43 TThSo Kilnhurst to Shellhaven empties which are being conveyed in 100 tonne tanks. The loco would have worked up from Ripple Lane, East London, the previous evening, on the 6E62 MWFo conveying the same tanks which are left at Croda overnight to allow for discharge. This BR Railfreight petroleum operation to South Yorkshire runs six days a week using the same Immingham loco. Since the opening of the new Swinton Curve all passenger trains now use the ex-Midland line between Aldwarke Junction, Swinton and Mexborough, thus leaving the ex-Great Central line between Aldwarke and Mexborough exclusively for freight traffic including the Silverwood Colliery MGR trains.

LOWER RIGHT: Not technically a freight train but an interesting picture of BR's Research Railway Technical Centre DRTC locomotive, 31970, at present stored unserviceable. The picture, taken on 2nd March 1990, shows 31970 in the red, blue and white livery of the Technical Centre, running south from Treeton Junction, near Tinsley Yard, on the freight-only ex-Midland main line between Rotherham Masborough and Chesterfield which avoids Sheffield Station, The ensemble is running as the 6Z31 special between Doncaster and Derby with a track-recording vehicle. In 1851 the Sheffield area was producing 86% of British Cast Steel. One hundred and forty years later however had seen an about-turn with vast amounts of steel now being imported into Britain, including shipments via rail to Sheffield! Thus over the past couple of years Tinsley Yard has seen a reduction in 'home grown' services and because of this has been heavily rationalised. It now plays host to mainly 'metals' sector diagrams delivering scrap to the now much reduced local steel industry. When Tinsley Yard was opened on 29th October 1965, it could handle 275 trains over any 24 hour period. The rusty sidings to the left used to service Orgreave Colliery and Coking Plant. Unfortunately the colliery closed some years ago and the coking plant succumbed in December 1990.

UPPER LEFT: With a mixture of engineers' wagons in tow, including four different designs of brakevan, 37407 *Loch Long*, pictured on 2nd March 1990 and then a member of Immingham's DCEA pool of Eastern Region Civil Engineer's locos, is traversing the freight-only line at Templeborough which runs between Tinsley Yard and Rotherham Central Station, the train being en route to Doncaster Wood Yard Civil Engineer's Depot. Since this picture was taken 37407 has been transferred back to Inverness where it was a member of the PISA pool, but recently has been sent south to Eastfield and has joined the FPAE, Petroleum fleet. 37407 had only recently been outshopped from Doncaster Major Depot when this picture was taken. Its time at Doncaster included an intermediate overhaul and repaint into Inter-City colours. In the background can be seen the Tinsley M1 viaduct along with the two redundant cooling towers which have become a local landmark.

ROTHERHAM

LOWER LEFT: A one time exclusively Southern Region shunting loco, 09013 unofficially named *Shepcote* and now a member of the Tinsley shunter fleet (FMST) is pictured approaching Ickles on the freight-only route between Rotherham Central and Tinsley Yard. The shunter, re-allocated firstly from Ashford, Kent, to Cardiff and then in October 1989 to Tinsley, is working the 9T38 trip from Rotherham Steel Terminal to Tinsley Yard and is conveying three BDA flat wagons loaded with steel slabs. The steel will leave Tinsley Yard on the 6076 to Sheerness and will arrive in Kent the following day. Rotherham forms the skyline to the picture, and the land to the right was once the site of a large steel complex demolished two years ago.

UPPER RIGHT: The buffers in Deepcar Exchange Sidings symbolise the end of the line for the once famous Woodhead route which lost its passenger services in 1970 and closed completely in July 1981. The line has now been lifted between Deepcar, Woodhead Tunnel and Hadfield from where there is a frequent 25kv electric service into Manchester Piccadilly. 37227, a Thornaby Metals loco, is working the local trip from Tinsley Yard on 16th March 1990, and is conveying three HEAs and two OCA open wagons for the UES complex at Stocksbridge. 37227 will have run round in Deepcar BR Exchange Sidings and will draw forward in order to propel the wagons into the UES private sidings. From here the works shunter at Stocksbridge will trip the cargo into the UES complex.

CENTRE RIGHT: Looking very much like a rural branch line scene, the location is in fact Deepcar on the erstwhile 1500dc Woodhead Trans-Pennine rail route. 37227, a Thornaby steel pool loco (FMTY) in steel sector livery, is pictured passing the ex-Great Central signal cabin with the 6T02 working from Deepcar Exchange Sidings to Tinsley Yard. The BDA bogie bolsters are conveying finished steel from the nearby United Engineering Steels (UES) complex at Stocksbridge whilst the POA wagons are carrying scrap bound for the British Steel processing plant at Aldwarke Junction located on the ex-Great Central route between Rotherham Central and Mexborough. In March 1990 BR acquired 181 POA scrap wagons from Standard Railfreight and these have now been reclassified as SSAs. The gabled station at Deepcar, once known as Deepcar for Stocksbridge, is 8¾ miles from Sheffield Victoria, closed on 4th January 1970 to passengers, and was built by the Manchester, Sheffield and Lincolnshire Railway Company which became part of the Great Central. The station is now a private residence as is Wortley further north along the line. Wortley Station once boasted a private waiting-room which was used exclusively by the Earl of Wharncliffe who lived nearby. The signal cabin at Deepcar is now a shunters' mess room and all signalling on 'the branch' is controlled by Sheffield Powerbox.

LOWER RIGHT: Looking somewhat 'worse for wear', the UES works shunter No. 35, built by the Yorkshire Engine Company in 1962, is pictured on 15th March 1990 having just tripped the VTG Ferrywagon and BDA flats up the 1 in 80 gradient from Stocksbridge works. The Ferrywagon is bound for Austria with export steel bars which will run via Tinsley Yard, and the BDAs are destined for British Steel at Scunthorpe. Samuel Fox opened his ironworks (now UES) at Stocksbridge in 1842 and by 1874 had put a Bill before Parliament to construct a railway line to connect his Stocksbridge Works with the main Manchester, Sheffield and Lincolnshire line at Deepcar. The line when laid ran for two miles west of Deepcar and became known as the Stocksbridge Railway, a private concern which it remains to this very day. It opened on 14th April 1877 and was used initially to transport iron from Fox's to Sheffield. However, when the station at Deepcar opened on 1st July 1888, Fox's workers could catch special trains which ran directly into the ironworks complex.

UPPER FACING: 37066, a member of Immingham's DCEA Civil Engineer's fleet, is pictured on 14th March 1990 before its repaint into the drab plain-grey general livery which BR have adopted for Engineer sector locos. It is seen in BR Standard rail blue colours and is working the 6G14 special past the now-closed Monckton Coking Plant. 37066 has a single HEA cripple wagon in tow from Grimethorpe Colliery, and is bound for Healey Mills Wagon Repair shops via Wakefield Kirkgate and Horbury Junction. Traffic on this truncated ex-main line is now reduced to the 6K82 Grimethorpe to Eggborough MGR coal working and the 6E83 sand train to Monk Bretton, both workings running daily except Saturday.

LOWER FACING: The driver of 56095 Harworth Colliery, a Toton FEDN pool loco, waits by the semaphore signals at Royston Junction with the 6K82 Eggborough to Grimethorpe Colliery empties on 15th March 1990. Emergency working was in force on the section of line between Oakenshaw South Junction and Grimethorpe Pit because vandals had removed the signal pulley wires from the semaphores rendering them inoperable. A pilotman had to join the driver from the nearby Royston Junction signalbox before the journey could commence down 'the branch'! The signal wire had been stolen on several occasions and a decision had been taken to work the mere two trains a day with a pilotman rather than to reinstate the signal wire only to see it stolen again over a weekend when this section of line is closed. Royston Junction is so named because of the branch which ran off the Midland line in this location to Dewsbury. This line has now been closed and lifted, putting many of the Royston signalbox levers out of use. Royston also boasted its own motive power depot and station up until 1967 when both closed. The shed was coded 55D and its allocation was exclusively freight engines, predominantly Stanier 8Fs which were used on heavy coal traffic. Even though the depot was on BR's Eastern Region its pre-Nationalisation origin was LMS, being situated next to the Midland main line, which is now just a shadow of its former self, with only two freight trains a day. A far cry from the day when the Thames-Clyde express used this prestigious route!

RIGHT: Stourton Freightliner Terminal, on the ex-Midland line at Hunslet between Leeds City and Normanton is playing host to 08661, a Neville Hill allocated shunter from the PNLA pool. Formally a Norwich engine it was transferred to Leeds after being one of the last 08s outshopped from Derby Works. The terminal handles three freightliners a day departing to Tilbury (4L56), Stratford (4L63), and Southampton (4O96) as well as arrivals from Felixstowe (4E50), Tilbury (4E65), Bescot (4E72) and Crewe (4E51) Up until 1967 Stourton was known to older enthusiasts as 55B, a sub-shed of Leeds Holbeck 55A. Its steam allocation numbered 25 in 1965 and all locos were of the freight type, including Stanier Class 8Fs and BR built 3MTs.

LEFT: Looking resplendent in ex-works condition, 37144, a member of Immingham's FABI Construction pool, just outshopped from Doncaster Major Depot, is pictured traversing the truncated ex-Midland main line near to Royston Junction with PAA sand hoppers. 37144 has been rostered for the 6E83 Company train from Middleton Towers (Kings Lynn) to Redfearn National Glass situated at Monk Bretton to the north-east of Barnsley. The ex-Midland main line, as can be seen by the spare ballast, used to carry quadruple track here and was a major passenger route between Leeds, Normanton and Sheffield. During the late 1970s it was truncated at Grimethorpe Colliery and the section of track between Houghton Main Colliery, now closed, and Wath was lifted. The signalman at Royston Junction box nicknamed this route the 'Victor Sylvester line' as in the dance leader's 'quick, quick, slow' routine, meaning that in its heyday of carrying express passenger trains, mining subsidence had reduced the line to many speed restrictions! 37144 will have worked double-headed from Middleton Towers to Doncaster Belmont Speedlink Yard with another Class 37. At Belmont the PAAs are split and tripped to two other glassworks in the area, namely Rockware at Kirk Sandall to the north-east of Doncaster, and the Co-op glassworks at Worksop, this working travelling via the ex-South Yorkshire Joint Railway system.

BELOW: With plenty of acrid exhaust, the driver of 47209 has just opened up the regulator after a signal check, and is joining the ex-Midland main line at Treeton Junction, east of Sheffield Midland with three POA scrap wagons forming the 6M69 from Tinsley Yard to Washwood Heath, Birmingham, the date being 17th May 1989. Most of the traffic from Tinsley Yard is now sponsored by the Railfreight Metals sector and handles scrap from the local steel industry, the majority of workings leaving from the west end of the yard. Since this picture was taken 47209 has gained *Herbert Austin* nameplates, Railfreight Distribution livery and sub-sector markings, being based in Tinsley's FDAT pool. The bridge abutment seen just to the right of 47209 used to carry a line into the nearby Treeton Colliery, which has now become an opencast site.

ABOVE: 08665, a long time resident of Immingham depot, and a member of the FMMI pool of shunters is pictured on 21st July 1987 in the heartland of the Associated British Port's owned Immingham Docks complex. 08665 was acting as the Transit Shed pilot, a duty which has since been withdrawn. The VDA vans are ready to be shunted into a Railfreight Distribution working bound for Doncaster. The Great Central Railway invested £2.6 million pounds in the building of the docks, mainly to export coal, 170 miles of track being laid, which today unfortunately is vastly reduced. The Railfreight arm of BR, notably the petroleum sub-sector, still has a vested interest in Immingham with 25 scheduled departures from Lindsey (Petrofina and Total) and Humber (Conoco) oil refineries which leave Immingham each weekday for destinations all over the BR network. The two oil refineries only became rail connected in 1970 when production began at the plants. Twenty-one years later in 1991 rail traffic from the two sites totals four million tonnes plus per annum.

RIGHT: A picture which I felt needed to be included, and one which illustrates part of Immingham MPD's past. For younger readers the Great Central Railway opened its steam depot at Immingham in 1912 to coincide with the recently completed docks area. However the pre-cast concrete coaling tower which is pictured was built by BR in the 1950s to replace an old wooden structure used by the Great Central Company. As can be seen it is still standing 25 years after the shed closed to steam traction. In 1966 much of the old steam depot, coded throughout its BR days as 40B, was demolished and a new purpose-built diesel depot was constructed on the site. Parts of the old fitting shop survived however and are still in use today, unlike the redundant coal stage! Today over 100 diesels are allocated to the modern depot, the majority belonging to the petroleum and metals sub-sectors. In addition to the diesel depot there is a wagon repair shop servicing the PTA tippler wagons which work the iron-ore traffic between Immingham and Scunthorpe. 08439 pictured left is long withdrawn and awaits a tow to the scrapyard.

BELOW: Passing the rather austere-looking signal cabin on the ex-Lancashire & Yorkshire line at Womersley Road, Knottingley, is 56123 *Drax Power Station*, a member of Toton's FEDN pool. Aptly enough 56123 is working the 6K89 Drax to Selby Drift Mine empties consisting of 36 HAAs. Selby Drift Mine at Gascoigne Wood was opened in 1984 and produces the largest output of coal, 180,000 tonnes per week, of any pit in the United Kingdom. The coal is destined for either Drax or Eggborough Power Station. Knottingley sees countless MGR trains per day carrying over half a million tonnes a week from 13 local pits to power stations. The depot at Knottingley has eighteen daily diagrams for which 22 Toton-based Class 56s from the FEDN pool are available. A and B exams are carried out at the depot but any other work is carried out by the parent depot, Toton. Wagons are also maintained at Knottingley and nearly 1500 HAAs are used to make up 39 sets, as this is the longest train length which can be accommodated in the pits and power stations of the Aire Valley.

FACING UPPER: 08743 is the Immingham Reception Siding's T82 trip pilot, the picture being taken on 3rd March 1990. In 1906 a line was constructed by the Grimsby and Immingham Light Railway Company, the six mile branch connecting, as the title suggests, the two ports, Immingham being the newer, opened in 1912, whilst Grimsby had been an important port as far back as medieval times. Today the line serves half a dozen Railfreight customers which are located between Pyewipe Road Level Crossing and Immingham East Junction. The Immingham Dock estate originally covered 1000 acres, 45 of which were water-served. The complex was opened by King George V on 22nd July 1912, the official sod cutting taking place six years earlier on 12th July 1906. Today Immingham handles the third largest tonnage of goods after Southampton and Dover, the main commodities being iron ore and coal. Fertilisers, timber, cars and chemicals are also handled, and recently a new Railfreight Distribution Freightliner service was commissioned between the docks and Leeds.

FACING LOWER: The City of Leeds forms the backdrop as 47286, a Tinsley FDBT Distribution loco, which is hit-listed at present, being overdue an F exam, propels its train of MSV wagons into Balm Road Ready Mixed Concrete (RMC) stone terminal after arrival from Peak Forest as the 6E17 SX working. It will depart later in the day as the 6M17 SX empties bound for Peak Forest. The method of unloading at Balm Road, which is opposite BR's Hunslet Yard, is very primitive. Mechanical diggers literally scoop the roadstone from the MSV wagons and deposit the material into lorries. Hunslet Yard, as can be seen by the empty sidings, doesn't generate the amount of traffic as in previous years, dealing mainly with local workings. These can include Railfreight Metals trips to nearby Whitehall Road or Railfreight Distribution traffic to Wakefield and Doncaster.

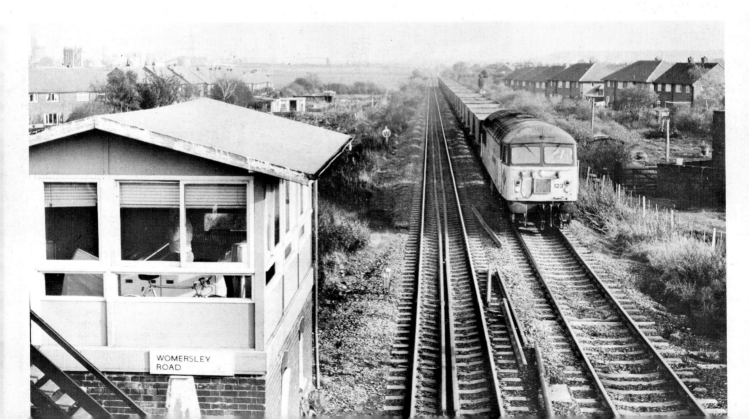

WOMERSLEY ROAD

GRIMSBY DOCKS

ABOVE: Grimsby Royal Dock is the location of this picture and 08665, an Immingham FMMI pool engine, is seen shunting stainless steel which has actually been produced in Sheffield but rolled into coil in Bremerhaven, Germany, to be sent back to Sheffield and Cardiff! The BVWs built in 1957, and capable of carrying 60 tonnes, are being used to transport the steel from the Royal Dock quayside to the BR Exchange Sidings located at West Marsh Yard. The BVWs were formally coded JVV and used extensively in South Wales. Grimsby had been an important port for many years. Today's dock was opened in 1852 and latterly belonged to the London and North Eastern Railway (LNER). It contained 139 acres of water and flourished with its fish and general overseas trade market. At the height of its fishing popularity BR despatched eight express fish trains a day to places as far apart as Manchester and London. However by the early 1960s road haulage had become more prominent and BR lost its fish traffic. Grimsby has boasted three stations, the Docks, the Pier and Grimsby Town, the last still open today for rail passengers. During 1976 the dock branch was scheduled for closure but a saviour came in the form of exported stainless steel work from Sheffield to West Germany, operating to this day and helping to keep this rail-connected dock as an important part of the BR freight network.

UPPER RIGHT: In happier times, 47402, withdrawn from BR operating stock on 19th December 1990, is pictured passing the Humber (Conoco) Oil Refinery at Immingham with the 6D71 Lindsey to Leeds working just two months before withdrawal from the FPXA, Class 60 Contingency Plan loco fleet, based at Immingham. The loco when pictured on 23rd October 1990 was still running in BR Standard Rail Blue livery and had by this time been relegated to just local oil duties mainly on Leeds workings to Hunslet East Oil Terminal, a far cry from the day it was employed on crack express services on the ECML. The withdrawal of 47402 has left just four 'Generators' in Capital Stock, namely 47401/413/417/418. 47401, the original D1500, the first member of the class, is to be found in the FPXA pool whilst 47413/417/418 are members of the IECA pool, Inter-City East Coast Main Line locos. 47401 is currently a preservation candidate, the Class 47 Locomotive Society having already raised £25,000 to secure the loco on withdrawal from BR for the enjoyment of future generations of enthusiasts. Note the two industrial shunters owned by the Humber Oil Refinery, sadly both out of use at the present time. 47402 was unusually reinstated at Immingham on 4th February 1991 into the IECA Inter-City pool.

LOWER RIGHT: With the surrounding ground covered in red dust, 37225 still in BR standard blue livery and 37275 in steel sub-sector Railfreight colours, both members of Immingham's FMYI fleet, are pictured leaving Immingham Iron Ore Terminal with the 13.55, 6T27 working conveying 21 PTAs to Santon Ore Terminal located at British Steel's Scunthorpe complex. Loading takes fifteen minutes at Immingham because three wagons can be accommodated at any one time. At Scunthorpe unloading is a little slower because each wagon is tipped separately. Ships arrive at Immingham Docks regularly with 75,000 tonne shipments of iron ore, at present imported from Australia and Sweden. This means that BR and the port handle five million tonnes of ore each year necessitating between sixteen and twenty services to Scunthorpe each day, including Saturdays.

ABOVE: 47231 *The Silcock Express*, a member of Tinsley's FDAT fleet, a Distribution loco, so technically operating the wrong type of traffic, is framed by the semaphore signals at Brocklesby Station Junction, and is leaving the freight-only line from Immingham with the 6D73 Lindsey to Leeds working on 23rd October 1990, conveying TEA oil tanks. Brocklesby Station is a red brick Jacobean-style building constructed in 1847, and includes a private waiting room built for Lord Yarborough, then the Chairman of the Manchester, Sheffield and Lincolnshire Railway Company. The station was also used by royalty calling at the nearby Brocklesby Hall. Inside there is ornate cornice work as well as the original chimney pieces, but the station, now no longer owned by BR, is in a sad state of disrepair and will cost several thousand pounds to repair. The station is still used by rail services on the Sheffield to Cleethorpes route.

BROCKLESBY JUNCTION

SCUNTHORPE

UPPER LEFT: On a misty winter's morning, 24th October 1990, 37083 eases through Scunthorpe Trent Yard, having just left the Anchor Exchange Yard with the 6J25 bound for Sheffield Freight Terminal carrying stainless steel bars on BDAs. 37083 still in BR Standard Blue Livery is a member of Thornaby's FMTY pool of locos. During 1990 freight handling in Scunthorpe has seen many changes. Scunthorpe West Yard was closed in March 1990. It had been rebuilt in 1971, and incorporated the hump system of sorting wagons, similar to the yard at Tinsley. Trent Yard, built during the 1960s, then had the majority of its traffic diverted to the West Yard. Also during the early 70s, British Steel had extended its system of private lines and laid tracks to a new section of sidings known as Anchor Exchange Yard. Although belonging to British Steel the yard was worked by BR. By 1986 Trent Yard had been mothballed, but it is now in the process of being upgraded, and with the forming of the Railfreight Steel sub-sector all steel traffic is now worked through the Anchor Exchange Yard within the British Steel complex. The yard sees about fifteen departures daily to locations which include Wolverhampton, Brierley Hill and Cardiff.

LOWER LEFT: 56085 in new two-tone Railfreight grey livery, but minus its coal sub-sector markings, is a member of Toton's FEDN fleet and has just propelled the 6T35 out of British Steel's Coal Handling Plant onto the down main line at Scunthorpe which is adjacent to Trent Yard. Prior to 1989 and the opening of the Coal Handling Plant, the majority of British Steel's coal supplies arrived from the west, Maltby and Thurcroft pits near Doncaster supplying the coal. Today most of the coal arrives from the east via Immingham Docks, usually having been imported from Canada. There remains just one working from the west to date, that being the 7D66 from Thurcroft Colliery. On arrival from Immingham, 56085 will have run round its load of 36 HAAs in order to draw into the Coal Handling Plant. Immingham supplies the British Steel complex at Scunthorpe with up to eight loads of imported coal each week day.

SKELTON JUNCTION

A poignant reminder of what many of BR freight-only routes may look like by the mid-1990s. The scene pictured here is Skelton Junction to the south-west of Manchester Piccadilly. Track recovery has only taken place at the junction with the Northenden to Navigation Road (Altrincham) freight and passenger-carrying line. The rusty rails in the foreground once carried freight traffic between Skelton Junction and Warrington Arpley Speedlink Yard, but because of the recession that hit Britain in the early 1980s, this eleven mile freight-only route was severed and closed on 7th July 1985. Britain in 1991 is again in a recession and, with the recent BR announcement that the Speedlink Network will be abandoned from 8th July 1991, the future does not bode well for other freight-only lines that still exist within the BR network.